D1520125

# Lessons from the
# Art of Kempo

## Subtle And Effective Self-Defense

# Lessons from the
# Art of Kempo
## Subtle And Effective Self-Defense

## Fred Neff
### Photographs by Bob Wolfe

**Lerner Publications Company • Minneapolis**

East DISCARD chool
Gresham, Oregon

The models who appear in this book are Richard DeValerio, Michael C. Wong, John Wong, Michelle Wong, Diane Wolfe, Bob Wolfe, Andre Richardson, James Reid, and Douglas Shrewsbury.

LIBRARY OF CONGRESS CATALOGING-IN-PUBLICATION DATA

**Neff, Fred.**
    Lessons from the art of kempo.

    Includes index.
    Summary: Examines the history, philosophy, and techniques of the
martial art known as kempo, or kung fu, and describes how it
may be used for self-defense.
    1. Kung fu–Juvenile literature. 2. Self-defense–Juvenile literature.
[1. Kung fu. 2. Karate. 3. Self-defense] I. Wolfe, Robert L., ill. II.
Title. III. Series: Neff, Fred. Fred Neff's secrets of self-defense.
GV1114.7.N44    1987        796.8′159        86-27867
ISBN 0-8225-1160-6 (lib. bdg.)

Copyright © 1987 by Lerner Publications Company

Manufactured in the United States of America

International Standard Book Number: 0-8225-1160-6
Library of Congress Catalog Card Number: 86-27867
2  3  4  5  6  7  8  9  10  97  96  95  94  93  92  91  90  89  88

*To my mother, Mollie Neff, whose optimism and creativity light up the life of everyone who knows her.*

# CONTENTS

"Fred, come up out of the basement, it's time to go to bed."

"Hurry upstairs, it's time for you to go to school."

"You'd better get up here quickly, it's time to go to work."

I heard similar statements to get me out of the basement many times in my youth. The attractiveness the basement held for me remained somewhat a mystery to my parents for years. Yet, as I look back, no other place was as much a haven from everyday cares and a training ground for the future. What did I do during those long hours?

The name of my activity in the basement is *kempo*, which means "fist way." From the time I first watched the art it fascinated me. Sometimes techniques were slow and beautiful. At other times they were lightning fast, so that I saw an endless stream of movement. Once I had seen kempo practiced, I was hooked on it.

Properly practiced, kempo can help the student think more clearly, and improve general health, strength, self-defense skills, and self-esteem.

One of the most interesting by-products of practicing kempo is an inner confidence that stands you in good stead at times of stress. I remember that before I took the bar exam to become a lawyer, I not only studied the law, but also trained very hard in kempo. The more I practiced my kempo techniques, the better I felt about my chances to do well on the test.

Mental attitude may play a larger part than physical conditioning in preparation for the hard tasks of everyday living. You might have to defend yourself against an aggressor on some occasion. Training in a martial art for that one occasion may take up more time than that one chance of a challenge merits. If, however, an art—like kempo—has a far broader application, not only preparing you for self-defense, but also for everyday living, then the time spent is well worth it. To me, kempo is not a fighting art as much as a way to enhance living.

When people hear the word *karate*, they think of a figure flying through the air with a kick, or breaking bricks. When *kempo* is mentioned, they think, "What is that?"

Kempo is an art of philosophy, physical culture, and self-defense that develops the body, mind, and spirit. It includes meditation, punching, striking, kicking, throwing, and locking techniques. Also included are dodges, blocks, and sticking techniques for tying up an opponent with his or her own arms. Kempo moves are both linear and circular, allowing for a smooth flow of action from soft to hard movement. There is a continuity of action that makes it exhilarating to practice, irresistible to watch, and difficult to defend against.

The ultimate aim of kempo practitioners is not only to grow in power, but to improve themselves and learn to live in harmony with others.

However, kempo teaches that at times you may have to defend against an aggressor, and that unless you know adequate techniques, you might be harmed. Kempo teaches not only how to efficiently protect yourself, but also how to flexibly combine techniques in a smooth, free-flowing action that seems almost effortless to the viewer.

Kempo practice can help students maintain health, learn self-defense, quiet the spirit and better understand themselves. That is why this art, based on ancient practices, still has relevance in the modern world. This book teaches some of the introductory lessons that will give you the skills and confidence to achieve the harmony and happiness that the kempo practitioners believe in and strive for in their practice.

The history of kempo is a fascinating one that has been obscured by time and shrouded by legend. Tradition has it that kempo was founded by the great Buddhist monk Ta Mo, also called Dhrumba or Bodharma, at the Shaolin Temple sometime between A.D. 516 and 528. In fact, it may have a much longer history.

Since ancient times, India has had a martial tradition. Even today in India, they practice the art of *kalaripayit*, which resembles certain Chinese kung fu styles. Early Buddhist monks from the warrior caste probably trained in martial forms similar to kalaripayit and took those arts with them and taught them in their travels. Some historians believe that other monks visited China long before Ta Mo. They could have taught the fighting arts of India to the Chinese. There were also trading caravans traveling from India to China, which may have had Indian guards with extensive knowledge of martial arts.

Travelers even before Ta Mo may have contributed to Chinese martial arts. It is important to understand that China has a very long history. The Chinese have known fighting arts since ancient times. Historians have found specific references to archery, fencing, and wrestling as far back as the period of 1122 to 255 B.C. Chinese culture and history is so sophisticated that some fighting arts were probably used long before this early period.

It is likely that Ta Mo did not bring martial studies to China, but rather introduced a new system of philosophy and physical culture. Today this school of thought is called Ch'an or Zen. The set of exercises Ta Mo introduced was designed to enhance health and spiritual growth. Out of his teaching also came a fighting art named after the temple in which it was taught. That art is known as Shaolin Temple boxing. After Ta Mo, the Chinese monks at the Shaolin Temple continued to practice and develop their art.

When people left the temple, they sometimes taught outsiders their martial art. When these outsiders practiced the art, they made changes or adaptations. In time, many forms of fighting, all called *ch'uan fa* (fist way), evolved throughout China. The term *kung fu*, sometimes translated as "learned man," has also been used to describe these martial arts. Chinese monks or merchants who went to other lands, such as the island of Okinawa and the Japanese islands, often brought their art with them. Japanese and Okinawans who visited China for trade or study were also exposed to ch'uan fa. They brought their knowledge back with them and taught it in their homelands. The Japanese refer to ch'uan fa as kempo. When Chinese fighting techniques were brought to Japan they were modified by the native art of jujitsu, which included extensive grappling techniques. As time went by, the word *kempo* began to refer to arts of self-defense that emphasized hand and foot attacks that were influenced by Chinese ch'uan fa. These forms of fighting were not necessarily direct descendants of a particular Chinese form, but a synthesis of various Japanese methods with Chinese ch'uan fa-type techniques. As a result, there are often many distinct differences between ancient Chinese arts of ch'uan fa and modern kempo systems.

From Japan, kempo has spread throughout the world. Some schools have added and adapted fighting techniques from the countries in which they are located. Today, there is not one form of kempo, but many. In general, however, kempo uses the whole body in smooth, free-flowing action for self-defense. The best kempo practitioners are ones who cultivate a balance in body, mind, and spirit that gives them the ability to live in harmony with others.

# *2*
# PHILOSOPHY

Kempo teaches that a person must have the proper attitude and philosophy to be successful at any endeavor. The important principles of the art that follow make a person not only more effective at self-defense but also happier. Kempo develops the whole person.

1. *Don't worry.* Instead, focus on the solution. Kempo practitioners believe that it is difficult to keep your mind on two things at the same time. Therefore, instead of worrying about a problem, think about a solution. You will find that you are more relaxed and more comfortable. An obvious by-product of this is that the solution you reach will end the need for further worry. For example, if you are faced with a bully, do not think about how he or she can harm you, but look for an opening for defensive action. This technique can be applied not only when you face an attacker in a self-defense situation, but in your everyday life as well.

2. *You can do whatever you believe is possible.* The kempo practitioner believes that human potential is so tremendous that no person works at his or her full ability. Many of us think that we are not able to do things and we thereby create our own inadequacy. You should realize that you are capable of great accomplishments if you do not worry, but concentrate all of your energy on improvement. Your only limitation is what you believe you can do. Confidence and good feelings will result from believing that you can do something and then taking action.

3. *Use the opponent's actions against him or her.* Any action creates a

weakness or an opening for counterattack. In a difficult situation, concentrate on the other person's opening or weakness and take advantage of it. Even an opponent's strength can be manipulated to turn it to your advantage. For example, it may be a frightening prospect when a very powerful opponent puts all of his or her weight behind a punch. The kempo practitioner would grab the punching arm and pull forward on it while stepping away. This would throw the attacker off balance, putting him or her in a precarious position. This principle will work not only in grappling, but in life in general.

4. *Concentrate on what you do well.* Too many times, people focus on what they do wrong and feel badly about it. You must learn to feel good about your potential, recognize your strengths, and use them whenever possible. The winner in any fight is the person who takes advantage of his or her strengths or special skills. For example, if you are good at punching, then do not be concerned that the other person is better at kicking. Instead, put the attacker in a position where he or she is unable to kick and you can use your punches. Again, this principle can be applied on a far wider scope than just fighting.

5. *Be flexible in your approach.* An oak that is stiff will break in a strong storm, while a palm tree will yield and survive. The philosophy of kempo teaches that a human being should be like a palm tree and learn to bend and adapt to new or difficult situations. One must not be stuck in a rigid mold and unable to respond or change direction. One of the greatest strengths of kempo fighting techniques is that they are so adaptable. You should learn to use those techniques that will work in a situation and discard anything that will not. For example, certain styles of fighting teach students to move straight in with a punch or kick to end the fight. This move can be dangerous because the attacker may not allow or be open to such an attack. A kempo practitioner learns to expect the unexpected, and varies the self-defense technique to fit the situation.

6. *Persevere.* Be persistent and you will dissolve any challenge. Many people give up far too early if they meet resistance. Kempo teaches that any resistance can be dissolved by patient and continual dedicated action. If you meet challenges flexibly and confidently while following a strategy or plan, you can meet any reasonable goal.

7. *Dedicate yourself to continual self-improvement.* Kempo philosophy teaches that knowledge is endless. The more one knows the more one realizes how little is known. Recognition of this fact should lead to a lifetime of study and dedication to self-improvement. Practitioners of

kempo never become conceited because they know that kempo is an endless way.

8. *See the advantage in adversity.* To the kempo practitioner the world is a beautiful and wondrous place. Every day is an experience that helps to develop character. You should not expect only smooth sailing. Kempo teaches you to accept the occasional storm as a chance to learn and to become stronger. Every crisis has two parts: danger and opportunity. If you do not despair, if you see the opportunity and work hard to overcome the difficulty, you will gain from every experience.

9. *Try to live in harmony with nature and its ways.* Kempo teaches that all living things have an important part in this world. Respect others and try to live in harmony with them. You must not allow pride to stand in the way of peaceful relations with others. The kempo practitioner strives to understand nature better, in order to live in closer harmony with it. This lifelong search rewards you not only with the continual gain of knowledge, but also with greater insight and better relationships. Fighting skills are to be used only when absolutely necessary. First, one must seek peaceful methods of resolving confrontations. If there is no way to avoid a fight, the kempo practitioner will accept that conflict is a part of nature and move to defend himself or herself.

Even then, he or she will use only as much power or violence as is necessary to contain the attacker's aggression.

10. *Practice loyalty.* Loyalty breeds loyalty and makes human relations meaningful. Some people believe in looking out for themselves alone and getting all they can from others. Kempo teaches that the more you appreciate others and offer loyalty where it is deserved, the better you will feel about yourself. Kempo practitioners value loyalty to family, teachers, friends, and employers.

Loyalty starts with your family. Each member of a family is different, yet if they work together they can accomplish what no one of them can do alone. Unity of action creates harmony and strength. Loyalty keeps humans together so they can accomplish greater things and improve themselves by learning from each other.

In kempo, the teacher is like a parent who lovingly guides the student. Kempo puts tremendous physical, mental, and emotional demands on its students. The dynamic learning process shapes the individual through challenge and continuous demands. The student emerges as a new and better person. Students who recognize the teacher's efforts and are loyal to him or her benefit tremendously. Their positive feelings toward the teacher act as an inspiration and guide throughout their lives.

# 3

# EXERCISES

In order to become physically fit, you must condition your body through exercise. Your exercises can combine a program of body-conditioning techniques and sports.

This chapter presents a program of exercise for beginning students. You should start by practicing these exercises daily for about twenty minutes. Gradually add more repetitions of each exercise as you become more fit. In this way, you can create a conditioning program that will meet your needs.

Wear loose, comfortable clothing when you exercise so that you can move freely. Remember to exercise slowly so you do not strain muscles. Never force any muscle—instead, stretch it.

## The Basic Neck-Flexibility Exercise

Stand with your feet spread slightly apart and arms hanging loosely at your sides. Turn your head slowly in a circle, tilting it as far as possible without strain. Return to your original position, then rotate your head in the other direction. Repeat five more times in each direction.

## Front-Bending Exercise

Stand with feet slightly apart. Bend down and reach for the ground with your fingers. Keep your legs almost straight as you do so. Return to starting position. Repeat five times.

## Basic Side Stretch

Stand erect with your feet apart. Place your left hand on your hip and reach and stretch with your right hand as far to your left as you can. Straighten up, then stretch to the right. Stretch to each side three times.

## Body-Twisting Exercise

Stand with your feet apart and your knees slightly bent. Hold your arm bent at the elbow at chest level. Twist at the waist as far as you can comfortably go to the left, then to the right. Repeat in each direction at least four times.

## The Basic Two-Leg Stretch

Stand erect with your feet apart. Slowly spread your feet farther apart. Stretch a little farther at each exercise session until you can lower yourself close to the ground. Not everyone needs to be able to touch the ground. Don't force it. Do this only once during each exercise session.

## The Wall Push-Up

Put your palms against a sturdy surface at chest height and then move your feet back about three feet. Bend your arms and bring your chest toward your hands until you feel tension on your lower legs. Hold for a count of at least ten.

## The Basic Sit-Up

Lie on your back with your knees bent and soles of your feet flat on the floor. Sit up and hug your knees. Lie down again and repeat the exercise slowly ten times without stopping.

# MEDITATION

Physical exercises combine with meditation to prepare a person for kempo practice. Calisthenics loosen the body and help work off stress or anxiety. Meditation helps clear the mind, relax the body, and make a person more receptive to learning. It is a tool that can be used not only to prepare for fighting but also to handle daily pressure. A person in a relaxed state of mind is able to think more clearly. You can meditate any time you want to relax.

There is nothing supernatural in meditation, so don't expect anything more than a gentle relaxation.

To meditate, simply follow the steps below.

1. Sit cross-legged in a quiet place, with your left leg crossed over your right and your hands in your lap. Hold onto your left thumb gently with your right hand.
2. Keep your upper body erect and relaxed.
3. At first, keep your eyes half open and concentrate on a spot directly in front of you. Later, you may close your eyes if that is more comfortable.
4. Let your body go loose.
5. Deeply inhale and hold for a count of four and then exhale through your mouth. Repeat at least five times.

After the deep-breathing procedure,

if you still have tension left, tense your toes for a count of two and then let go. Imagine a gentle, relaxing heaviness beginning to flow upward from your toes. As the heaviness moves through your body, each part of you should feel heavy, relaxed, and comfortable. Once you have brought the feeling of heaviness up to the head, close your eyes and concentrate on the number one by repeating it over and over again. Whenever your mind wanders, simply bring it back to the number one. Don't try to achieve anything. Simply relax and let go. After a short while you will reach a state of gentle relaxation and feel good mentally and physically.

To end your meditation, simply open your eyes slowly and then sit for a couple of minutes to allow your body to adjust back to its normal state. You will find that when you stand up, your mind and body will be relaxed and ready to handle the rigors of training and other challenges.

# COMMON QUESTIONS

Students are always curious when they start to learn the art of kempo. This chapter answers several commonly asked questions about the philosophy, history, and techniques of kempo. The answers will help you understand this ancient art.

## 1. Why is kempo called an endless way?

There are several reasons for the term *endless*. Kempo philosophy teaches that knowledge is without end. There are endless benefits from studying the art. There are endless variations of the application of the techniques. The combinations of movements flow in an endless stream. Kempo practitioners aim to develop a smooth, endless flow in thought and action, so they have an effective response for any situation.

## 2. If kempo is so effective, why isn't it as well known as karate?

The words *karate* and *kempo* are simply general descriptions of a type of self-defense. Each of these martial arts has techniques in common with the other so that someone without knowledge might think they are the same. Fast, flowing hand techniques have often been called karate when in fact they belonged to kempo. For

many years, kempo practitioners did not clearly define their art, allowing other people to call it karate. As kempo practitioners are becoming better known, the art is becoming better recognized. Soon, people will know what kempo is, even though the uninitiated will never be certain whether or not they are seeing karate or kempo.

### 3. I have heard that some fighting arts are "hard" and others are "soft." What does this mean? And which best describes kempo?

In soft arts many of the movements are circular. They seem to flow from one to the next. Power comes from proper mental preparation and deep breathing.

Hard techniques are powerful techniques that seem abrupt and use an economy of motion. Most attacks are linear— straight out, and straight back. The power of the hard techniques comes from body mechanics, muscle power, and physical conditioning.

Many karate styles are characterized as hard. Kempo, on the other hand, is both circular and linear. It is a system of fighting that combines hard and soft movements. This gives it tremendous flexibility and makes it effective for many people.

### 4. Does kempo teach a special view of self-defense?

Yes. Kempo teaches that self-defense is a part of living: a way of dealing with conflict. Each individual is important, so kempo teaches how to deflect an attacker's aggression or violence without destroying the person. The kempo practitioner learns to move an attacker in a way that is consistent with nature. Each technique must be not only efficient, but consistent with nature's rules.

### 5. How long does a person have to practice to become a kempo expert?

To become skillful in kempo takes many years because one has to learn to use each part of the body efficiently and to move with the greatest effectiveness. Your reward is not necessarily the achievement of expert status, but the enjoyment of practice on a daily basis. However, it is not necessary to spend years practicing in order to become effective in kempo. If you practice at least three times a week for a couple of years you will develop effective techniques.

### 6. How should I prepare myself physically for kempo training?

First, get a medical checkup. Then begin to prepare your body with calisthenics and slow stretching exercises that will fully condition each of the major areas of the body. Exercise which will improve your endurance, such as swimming or bicycling, should also be included in your training. Do these endurance exercises a minimum of three days a week. Further, it is highly recommended that you try to walk at least a half hour every day. Many people fail to realize the many benefits of a brisk walk. It not only helps your wind, but gently massages most of the major parts of the body as you move. These various forms of exercise will be almost as important in your development of skill and effectiveness as the actual fighting techniques. Poor physical condition has often lost a fight for someone who had the knowledge, but not the ability to use it because of weakness.

### 7. What happens if I try to defend against a bully who has studied karate?

In any confrontation the key considerations are self-confidence, clear thinking, skill, timing, speed, conditioning, and persistence. A bully who has studied karate will not necessarily have more of these variables in his or her favor. If your confidence is great and you keep a clear head, then your chances are very good.

Karate styles vary tremendously. Some are very similar to kempo. In fact, some people call kempo a type of karate. More important than the style you know, is how well you use it. Practice daily to develop confidence and skill, and you need never fear any bully. The very fact that bullies try to prove themselves by picking on someone who appears to be weaker shows that they are missing the most vital factor of self-defense: self-confidence.

### 8. Are there any general tips that will be helpful in kempo training?

1. Keep an open mind toward fighting techniques. Consider it and try it —don't just reject it.
2. Concentrate totally on what you are doing, and do not be distracted by other matters.
3. Stay loose so that you do not wear yourself out and can move faster. The only time tension is necessary is the moment before the impact of a punch.
4. Use proper form with effective movement. Proper form is the essence of good self-defense.
5. Never hold your breath or strain your breathing when training. Relax and breathe properly and your techniques will be more powerful, yet you will not tire as quickly.
6. Breathe deeply. Breathe so that your lungs fill completely, not just in the upper chest. Try to breathe from an area approximately 2 to 2½ inches below the navel.

### 9. Do you have any suggestions on how I can improve my health?

Kempo is an excellent tool for improving one's health. As part of your training, try to:

1. Get enough sleep. This will keep muscles rested, loose, and pliable. Do not exercise strenuously when you are extremely tense or tired.
2. Walk as much as possible. Walking is an excellent general conditioner as well as a warm-up for training.
3. Eat lightly so as to not overburden the body. Refrain from eating for

at least one hour before training. Give your body proper nutrition—avoid sweets and junk foods.

4. Drink a lot of water daily. This helps lubricate your system, clear your skin, and energize you.

5. Avoid doing anything, including kempo, to excess. Kempo teaches moderation.

6. Exercise at least three times a week. Stretch and condition the body slowly, and gradually increase the intensity and duration of your exercises.

7. Work different muscles at alternate workouts so each muscle group can rest.

8. Avoid worrying. If you can, do something immediately about any problem. Stress and anxiety can wear you out. When you take action, fear, worry, and anxiety soon dissolve.

9. Use meditation as a tool to cut down on anxiety and stress.

10. Set aside times to be alone and relax. Plan activities that you can look forward to participating in.

## 10. I have heard a lot about the development of extraordinary power in certain styles of kempo. How is this brought about?

Both karate and kempo teach that extra power can be generated through *ki*. The development of inner strength through proper body movement, breathing, and unification of mind and body through spiritual growth is often called ki. The attitude and energy of ki add force to your techniques and improve your health. It takes many years to develop ki. If you want to cultivate this force, you should study under a qualified martial arts instructor. Ki is a significant factor in making martial arts a helpful and unique contribution to human knowledge.

## 11. How do I find a good kempo class that will satisfy my needs?

First, decide what you are seeking in a martial art. Ask yourself what you want to get out of the class, and then view a number of classes in different martial arts to see how they fit your needs. Martial arts differ in techniques, philosophy, rules, and even objectives. Not all teachers, even those of the same art, run their classes the same way or perform all techniques in the same manner. Keep in mind that some kempo systems are a synthesis of several methods of self-defense. Modern kempo training often has sporting aspects for fun and recreation. In picking a school, try to find out if they emphasize sporting competition and, if so, how the contests are conducted. If possible, you should view karate, kempo, and ch'uan fa classes in order to select the art that best fits your needs.

*6*

# BODY POSITIONS
# AND MOVEMENT

## STANCES

Stances are special standing positions that are used both in practicing kempo and in real self-defense situations. Some stances are defensive: they give your body stability and make it difficult for an opponent to throw you or knock you off balance. Other stances are offensive: they give your body flexibility to initiate attacks.

In addition to learning the stances, you must also learn how to move in an efficient and effective manner for self-defense. This chapter describes the best stances and the most commonly used movements in the practice of kempo.

The description of each stance includes a range of permissible placements for your feet. Generally, the farther apart you spread your feet, the more stability you have—and the

less mobility. You should practice each stance at the most comfortable position for you within the range of foot placements suggested for that stance. Your body build will determine the comfortable distance between the feet.

## Natural Stance

The natural stance is often used to stand at attention or to begin the other stances. When a fight starts, you may be caught in a natural stance and move into one of the other stances. However, you may have to launch an attack from a natural stance when there is no time to adjust your position. Certain throwing techniques are begun from this stance so it may be the best stance to take if the attacker is off balance.

To assume this stance, face your opponent and stand with your feet two to six inches (5 to 15 centimeters) apart. Keep your shoulders relaxed, and let your arms rest comfortably at your sides. Your back should be straight, and eyes focused on your opponent.

---

## Back Stance

The back stance is a defensive position. It is excellent when an attacker is lunging at you. A large part of the body weight is carried on the rear leg. Because of the strong rear support, this stance is stable and therefore a good stance for blocking. The forward leg has very little weight on it so front kicks can easily be used. Stand with one leg in front of the other so that the feet are approximately one and a half to two shoulder-widths apart, depending on whether stability or mobility needs to be emphasized. The rear leg should be deeply bent and carry about seventy percent of the body weight. The forward leg should be slightly bent

and carry the rest of the weight. The hands can be held in several positions. The low level position is most common.

## Front Stance

This is an excellent stance from which to begin attacks, and it allows for very fast forward movements. To assume this position, stand with your feet a little more than shoulder width apart. Your knees should be slightly bent with most of your weight on the forward leg. Most right-handed practitioners prefer to have their left foot forward; this allows them to use their weaker left arm and leg to keep the attacker away and save their right for more powerful punches and kicks. If you are left-handed, however, it would be better to have your right foot forward. Whether right or left-handed, you should practice your stance both ways so that you can defend yourself naturally no matter how you are standing.

The hands can be held in several positions as discussed below. The forward hand is commonly used for lead-in techniques to create openings for the powerful techniques that are thrown from the other side of the body. The basic low hand position is shown in the illustration.

NOTE: Unless otherwise specified, the left foot will be forward and the right foot in the rear on all illustrated techniques.

## Horse Stance

The horse stance can be oriented to the front, side, or on a slight diagonal to the opponent. A person can easily change from this stance to any of the other fighting stances. It can be a defensive stance, and powerful hand attacks can easily be thrown from this stance.

To assume a front horse stance, position your feet as though you were riding a horse, with your toes turned slightly inward. Your feet should be one and a half to two shoulder-widths apart. The torso should be erect and your weight evenly distributed over your feet.

Hold your hands in fists, palm up, slightly above the hips. Although this hand position is used when practicing this stance, it is not a common hand position in actual combat. This hand position is excellent for the practice of certain hand blows, but it does not provide an effective guard position.

The illustrations show the same stance in the side-facing and diagonal horse stance variations.

## HAND POSITIONS

There are three basic ways that the hands can be held in any of the stances. They are low guard, mid-guard, and high guard.

The best practitioners change hand positions as they move to keep the opponent confused and to best use their hands in each situation. Practice one guard first, and after you are comfortable with it, learn another.

Always consider your distance from an opponent when adjusting your hand guard position. When you are at close range, your head and chest are easy to hit, and a high guard position might be most useful. If your attacker throws mostly head-level kicks from further away, a high guard hand position may be best. If you are at long range, a low guard may be appropriate because your lower body is more easily hit.

## Low Guard

Hold your hands in fists at approximately hip level. Keep your elbows against your ribs to protect them. This guard lets you protect your groin and lower stomach while keeping your hands in a position from which you can throw very quick reverse and lunge punches. Sometimes you may hold the forward hand open to protect the lower part of the body. Traditionally, kempo practitioners keep one arm in front of the groin to protect it while throwing kicks.

## Mid-Guard

Both hands are held at approximately chest level with the hands open and the palms facing outward. Keep your elbows pointed in. Occasionally you may make the rear hand into a fist, keeping the front hand open for blocking or grabbing. The advantage of the mid-guard position is that it allows you to move quickly to protect your head or your lower body. In the mid-guard position, the open hands are more easily able to parry attacks, grab the aggressor's body, and launch open hand blows.

## High Guard

This position is excellent for quick hand maneuvers, yet lets you protect the upper body. Hold your elbows against the ribs with the forward fist at shoulder level and the rear fist a little higher—just below the ear. Point your chin down toward the chest to protect it. This guard is useful against a high kicking or punching attack.

## MOVEMENT

Kempo teaches that movement is one of the best tools for defense. A moving target is difficult to gauge and still harder to hit. Beginning kempo students practice changing from stance to stance as a type of subtle movement. To cover larger distances, however, other types of movement must be used.

Movement in kempo can be either straight or circular. A straight attack is used when you see a clear opening and you have no fear that your opponent would exert superior force in an exchange of blows. Circular movements are preferred because they keep you at an opponent's side or back, making you hard to hit. In a real confrontation, you would combine straight and circular attacks in order to respond to the opponent's moves and to employ your strategy. A kempo practitioner who can change stances, move, and dodge, has an effective arsenal for both offense and defense.

## Single Step

You can use the single step in any fighting stance. It is a very common movement because it allows you to cover a fairly large distance quickly. To perform a single step, start in a natural stance. Lift the stepping foot slightly off the ground. Quickly move the foot forward or backward and set it down. Make sure that your other foot, which serves as a pivot, is firmly on the ground. You must maintain proper posture and balance throughout the movement. Use this step to advance for an attack, to put your weight behind an attack, to dodge, or to counter a quick retreat.

## Slide Step

The basic slide step lets you cover short distances quickly. This is the most often used movement in a fight because it is fast and well-balanced. It can be used in any fighting stance. To move forward, slide the front foot forward. Next, slide the rear foot until you have regained your original stance. Maintain your fighting stance and your balance as you move. To move backward, slide the rear foot backward, then follow with the other foot.

## Side Step

Sidestepping lets you avoid a punch or kick above the waist. It is a very good dodge for an unexpected attack. Stand in a natural stance or a front stance. Quickly step to the side with one foot, simultaneously bending your body in the same direction. Shift most of your weight to your stepping foot once it is set. Bring up the hand on the stepping side, palm outward, and prepare to counterattack with the other hand. Counterattack immediately after the attacker's blow passes.

## Circle Step

Circle an opponent to keep him or her off balance and to let you get at your opponent from the side or back. A circular movement can confuse an opponent so that he or she is unable to mount an attack. It lets you handle much larger and more powerful attackers by preventing them from bringing their power to bear upon you. The circle step is best done from the horse stance or the front stance.

Move the forward foot four to eight inches (10 to 20 centimeters) to the right or left, depending on which direction you want to go. Then use the forward foot as a pivot to swing the rest of the body in the desired direction. When the pivot is complete, make sure that the rear foot is firmly on the ground. You should end in a strong fighting stance.

## Cross Step

Cross-stepping can quickly move you a long distance to the right or left. It often confuses an aggressor, making it difficult for him or her to predict what you will do next. Cross-stepping is done most successfully from the horse stance. To move to the left, lift your right foot and move it to the left side of your left foot. At this point, your knees should be bent and your feet crossed with the right foot in front. Next, move the left foot a large step farther to the left. To move to the right, reverse these movements.

# 7

# SENSITIVE SPOTS ON THE BODY

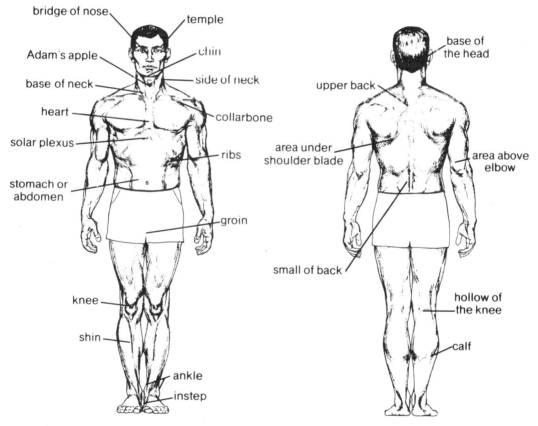

Certain parts of the human body are extremely sensitive to pain while others can take great punishment. A hard punch or kick to the attacker's body is not a guaranteed end to a fight. You usually must hit a pain-sensitive area to finish a fight.

The two diagrams point out the sensitive areas of the human body at which all blows should be aimed.

# 8

# HAND TECHNIQUES

Kempo offers many different hand techniques. Each has its distinctive strengths. However, a few hand techniques are used far more often than others, and these common maneuvers are included in this book. These techniques are the core techniques of kempo, and even the most skilled practitioners use them most of the time.

Each fighting technique sets up an opponent for the next. If one technique does not stop the fight then the next one might. However, once the aggressor is stopped, you should end your attack.

Your hand position will depend upon your stance and upon the situation. The punches and strikes taught in this chapter are mostly shown as being launched from either a low guard or high guard position, although with some adjustment you can launch the techniques from any of the guard positions. Because your hand position will vary, depending upon your movement and your opponent's actions, all types of blows should be intermixed in the combinations that you practice.

A general rule for all punches is that you don't tighten your fist or fingers until the last second before impact. Keeping your hand loose speeds up your blow and keeps you from tiring as quickly. Tightening it at the last moment adds snap to the blow, prevents injury to your hand or fingers, and helps focus the technique.

The illustrated starting positions for the blows were chosen because each is the easiest starting position for that particular hand technique. After learning the technique as shown, practice until you can use it smoothly and efficiently in a variety of body positions. Speed, timing, distance, and coordination are all important elements of a successful blow.

## The Basic Forefist Punch

A forefist punch is a straight punch. It is generally thrown from a horse stance or with the forward hand from any other stance.

Begin in a horse stance. Bring the punching hand to your hip in a loose fist, palm facing upward. The other hand should stretch out, fingers slightly bent, ready to block. Pull back the outstretched hand as your punching hand shoots up and out. Turn your fist as you punch so that when the punch lands your knuckles face upward. The elbow of the punching arm should pass close to the body. Your body and fist should be loose until a moment before impact, when you should tense slightly to focus the technique. After impact your body should be relaxed.

## The Reverse Punch

This powerful punch uses a full hip pivot for power in delivery. It is thrown from the same side of the body as the rear foot.

Begin in the basic front stance. Lower your rear hand to hip level, palm up. Twist your hips as you shoot your arm forward. Turn your fist so that your knuckles are facing up upon contact. As your punching hand shoots out, your forward hand should be pulled down to hip level, palm up. The countermovement of one arm pulling back as the other shoots out adds extra power to the technique.

For added stability and power, keep both feet firmly on the ground while punching. For greater reach but less stability, lift your rear heel off the ground as you punch. If you do lift your heel, make sure to keep sufficient weight on your rear foot. Practice this punch with the rear heel both on the floor and off so that you can use either variation for maximum stability or reach.

## The Lunge Punch

This very powerful punch not only puts tremendous force behind a blow, but also covers a great deal of distance. As you punch, you step forward. The added weight and force of the torso moving forward puts power into the technique. It is a good exercise to practice lunge punches with alternate hands. Another variation that can be useful in a real self-defense situation is to follow a lunge punch with a reverse punch. This simple combination is often used to close distance with an attacker.

Begin in the front stance. Lower your rear hand to hip level, palm up. Step forward with your rear foot. As your stepping foot passes your stationary leg, your punch should start to move toward its target. As your foot lands in the front, the punch should land with the knuckles facing up. While the punching arm moves out, the other arm should be pulled down to hip level, palm up, to add extra force.

# The Spring Punch

This punch is very good for closing the distance between you and an attacker very quickly. It can be extremely effective. When the spring punch is a surprise attack it can take the fight out of your opponent. Be ready to follow this punch with additional techniques, such as the basic forefist punch. The basic spring movement with the legs can be used any time you want to close the distance to an attacker very quickly. Practice combining the movement with other hand techniques such as the driving punch or the palm-up punch.

Start in the front stance. Lift your front foot to step forward and push strongly forward with your rear leg. As you are moving, pivot your hips to generate power for your reverse punch. As your front foot touches the ground your punch hits its target. Timing and a strong springing action of your legs are keys to the delivery if this punch is to have power. You should travel approximately a foot (30 centimeters) toward your opponent as you punch.

A variation of this technique is known as the *leaping punch*. From any stance, leap forward in the air and punch with what was formerly the rear hand as you come down. This technique has great power and if used sparingly can catch an opponent by surprise.

## The Vertical Punch

In the vertical punch, the hand shoots out from the shoulder so that your knuckles form a vertical line when the punch lands, with the thumb side of the fist facing up. Use this technique when an attacker is very close and you need a quick punch. The main difference between the vertical punch and the ordinary forefist punch is the amount of turn in the punch. The ordinary punch or reverse punch rotate fully, from palm up to palm down, but the vertical punch uses only a partial turn. You can either fold the thumb over the fingers or bend it down on top of the fist.

Assume the front stance. Move your rear fist, palm up, to hip level. Twist your hips as the punching arm shoots up toward the target. At the same time, pull the other hand down to hip level, palm up. Just before contact, twist your fist so that the thumb faces upward when hitting the target. The vertical punch can be thrown with the forward hand like a forefist punch, with the rear hand like the reverse punch, or with a step forward like a lunge punch. For more penetration, extend the middle knuckle as shown.

## The Driving Punch

This extremely fast technique can be used as a lead technique. You can use it to keep the opponent away or off balance. It can confuse the opponent or set him or her up for another, more powerful technique. Add power by combining it with the slide step.

Take a high guard stance. Quickly shoot your forward fist forward, twisting it so the knuckles are on top upon impact. After hitting the target, bring your fist loosely back to the guard position. Do not stiffen up the arm as you recoil. Stay loose enough to quickly follow through with another punch if necessary. Before launching the punch, keep your elbow close to your body for maximum power and protection.

## The U Punch

The U punch is excellent against an attacker who covers up very well with blocking. It allows you to strike simultaneously at two places on the body. As a result, it is difficult to block.

Assume a diagonal horse stance. Shoot your forward hand out in a palm-up punch to the opponent's stomach while you throw a high reverse punch to the opponent's head with the other hand. Both punches should be almost in a direct line in front of your body. As you punch, lean your body slightly forward into the attack. Tense your chest muscles to focus the punch.

47

## The Rear Quarter-Turn Horizontal Punch

This is an excellent, quick, powerful punch thrown from a high guard stance. It is similar to the reverse punch, but the fist starts from a higher position and it allows more reach since the heel of the rear foot lifts as you punch.

Take a high guard stance. Rotate your right hip forward, and as it moves shoot your right fist forward. Twist your wrist a quarter turn so that the knuckles are on top upon impact with the target. As you punch, pull your left hand back slightly and let your right heel rise for maximum reach. When you need to cover a shorter distance, do not raise your heel.

## The Palm-Up Punch

The palm-up punch is useful when the opponent is very close. It can be equally effective from any stance, and can be thrown with either the front or the back hand. To execute the technique, turn toward your opponent as you bend your knees slightly. Pull the punching hand down so that the fist is just slightly above the hip, palm facing up. Drive the punching arm out as you push your legs upward.

## The Circle Punch

A circle punch is slower than a straight punch and can be more easily blocked. Therefore it is most effective when the attacker is first distracted by another technique. This punch is generally used when the opponent is very close. It can also be started as a fake punch to draw out an opponent.

Shift your weight onto your front leg as your rear hip twists forward. As your body turns, throw the rear fist from the shoulder in a short arc. The fist should hit the attacker's side with the thumb facing up. It is very important to put all of your weight behind this punch. Immediately after impact, shift back into your original position. The circle punch can also be thrown with the forward arm.

## The Backfist Strike

The backfist strike, like the driving punch, is very useful for setting up an opponent and keeping him or her off balance. It is very difficult to block when executed properly. You can use this strike to close in quickly on an attacker by combining it with the slide step.

Pull your arm back so that you feel a slight tension at the crook of your arm. Do not stiffen, but coil like a spring. Straighten your elbow as your fist moves forward. The back of the fist should strike the attacker. Immediately after contact, snap your fist back into position to be ready for additional blows. Keep your fist loose until just before impact.

## The Open-Hand Strike

The open hand strike is especially useful for hitting an aggressor's temple, neck, or ribs. It can be performed from any stance and from several different angles. When doing this technique, be sure to hit the opponent with the soft outside of your hand. Make sure that your fingers are tightly squeezed together and your thumb is folded downward to prevent injury to your hand.

### A. The Inside Open-Hand Strike

The inside strike is often performed from the front stance. Bring your striking hand across your body, up next to your ear, with the palm facing the head. Your other hand should be in front of you with the palm facing the opponent, ready to block or parry. Swing your striking hand forward, twisting your wrist so that the palm faces down and the outside edge of your hand strikes the target. At the same time, bring your other hand back to your side. Remember that bringing one hand back as the other one shoots forward adds power to the striking arm.

### B. The Outside Open-Hand Strike

Begin in a mid-guard position. Lift your rear hand up close to your ear with your bent elbow pointing to the side. Twist your rear hip forward as you swing your hand in an arc toward the target. Your elbow should be slightly bent as the edge of the hand hits the target with the palm facing upward.

## The Ridge-Hand Strike

This strike is used to hit sensitive areas such as the side of the opponent's body, head, or neck. It is generally a follow-up to another technique or a counter after a block. It can be faked to set up the opponent for another technique or to leave an opening for a specific counterattack.

Assume any stance with one foot in front of the other. Hold your striking hand across your body, palm open and with the thumb pressed tightly against the palm. Swing this hand toward the target. Snap the striking hand outward so that the area of the hand next to the thumb hits the target, palm up.

## The Hammer Strike

This can be a very powerful blow, and you can execute it with either hand. As with the circle punch, it is easier to counter than a straight technique. When you are close to an attacker, you should only use this strike as a follow-up.

Cock your rear fist by raising it slightly. Shift your weight over your front leg as you twist your rear hip forward and bend your rear knee. As your shoulders become square with your opponent, your fist should thrust out in a small downward arc so you strike the target with the side of your fist opposite your thumb. The arm must be loose until the moment of impact so that there is a quick snap in the lower arm as the blow reaches the target.

## Basic Elbow Strike

The elbow strike is used to deal with an attacker who is close to you. You can throw it at an opponent from various angles. Make sure you are within striking distance of an opponent before trying it, and hit quickly. The force behind the elbow strike comes from twisting the hip into the strike as well as the upward motion of the knees. While executing an elbow strike, keep the other arm across the center of your body to protect against a counterattack.

### A. The Forward Strike

Begin in a mid-guard or high guard position. Twist your rear hip forward as your elbow moves directly toward the target. The arm should twist slightly at the wrist so that when the elbow strikes the target, your palm is facing downward.

### B. The Sideward Strike

Begin in a side-facing horse stance. Draw your hand across your body, palm up. Drive your elbow toward the attacker as your wrist twists so that the knuckles are facing upward when your elbow makes contact.

## C. The Upward Strike

Begin in a mid-guard position. Drive the elbow of your rear arm upward to the target. Upon impact the thumb side of the fist should be facing downward.

## D. The Backward Strike

This elbow strike can surprise an opponent and catch him or her off guard. Your elbow should hit the attacker's face, chest, or stomach. To execute the strike, swing your hip and elbow to the rear.

Kempo teaches that the hands and feet should move together for effective self-defense. Although there are many kicking techniques in kempo, four basic kicks can cover each direction. Together with the following auxiliary kicks, they form the core of kempo kicking techniques. At first you should practice kicking techniques by themselves to master the proper form. As you become more confident and capable you should add kicks to your practice of punching techniques. The better kempo practitioner is one who learns to work the hands and feet together in smooth-flowing combinations.

In a fight, kempo kicking techniques are usually thrown very quickly to the opponent's legs or lower body. Kicks are rarely thrown above chest level because the higher the kick, the more likely the kicker can be thrown off balance. As a beginner, you should focus on form and on learning techniques that you can throw quickly and powerfully at easily accessible targets. High kicks can come later.

The kempo kicking techniques that follow are fast, powerful, and effective.

Practice the first five kicks with two different finishing moves: returning to the cocked, ready-to-kick position, and setting your foot back down immediately as you return to a balanced stance. Then you will be able to either throw several kicks with the same leg, or immediately follow a kick with a different technique—whichever the situation requires. Which finishing move you use is a strategic decision.

## Front Kick

This kick can be thrown with either the front or the rear leg. Each has its advantages. A front kick from the forward leg is fast and is an excellent lead into another technique. It can be used to keep the opponent at a distance, or even to close with an attacker. A kick from the rear leg is good for powerful attacks to the opponent's body.

To execute a front kick begin in a fighting stance. Bend your kicking leg as you lift your knee towards your chest. Bend your toes back so they will not be injured when your foot hits the target. Quickly snap the kicking leg forward and hit the target with the ball of your foot.

## Round Kick

The round kick is excellent for surprising an attacker because it hits unexpectedly on the side of the body.

Begin in the basic front stance. Shift your weight to the front leg and swing your back leg around toward the attacker. The leg should be bent at the knee and held away from the body parallel to the ground. As the leg swings around the side of your body, snap it outward and hit your target with the ball of your foot. You can also bend the foot back and hit with your instep.

## Back Kick

The back kick is used to defend against attacks from the rear. It can be used in combination with other kicks when you need to throw a blow but your back is turned toward the aggressor. You must maintain proper balance throughout the kick so that you generate enough power.

Begin in a front stance. Turn your head so that you can see behind you. Bring your rear leg forward and lift it up toward the chest. Thrust the kicking leg straight back and strike your target with the heel of your foot. Always be ready to follow up a back kick with hand defenses if necessary.

## Side Kick

The side kick can be used to start an attack or to keep the opponent away. This kick covers a long distance so that you can sometimes hit the attacker with it even though the person cannot reach you with his or her hands.

To execute the side kick, start in a side-facing horse stance. Bend your knee and lift your leg into a cocked position. Thrust your leg out so that the heel of the foot hits the target.

After you become accustomed to the side kick, try beginning in a natural stance and executing the kick smoothly and quickly. Make sure to return your foot to the ground as soon as you have kicked. When you can return your leg to the ground immediately, your kick will be faster and more difficult to block, and you will have greater protection against being unbalanced.

## Crescent Kick

The crescent kick is an excellent technique for striking an aggressor's ribs and chest or for blocking an aggressor's attacks.

Begin in either a forward stance or a side-facing horse stance. Bring your rear leg forward and strike the aggressor with the sole of your foot. Remember to turn your toes upward so that they will not be injured when you kick. An ideal way to practice this technique is to hold your forward hand, open, in front of you. Kick so that you slap your hand with the bottom of your foot.

## Spinning Back Kick

The spinning back kick is an unusual technique that often catches an attacker by surprise. This kick is most often used to strike an aggressor's stomach or chest. It should only be used when the opponent is retreating and there is plenty of room for you to maneuver.

To begin the kick, start in a side-facing horse stance or front stance. Pivot on your front foot and swing your body backward toward the aggressor. As your back becomes squared with the opponent, lift your kicking leg at the knee and turn your head so you can see the aggressor over your shoulder. When you can clearly see the target, thrust your kicking leg out just as you would in a back kick, and hit the aggressor with the heel of your foot. Recoil your kicking leg and then lower your foot to the ground if no further kick is necessary.

## Spinning Side Kick

The spinning side kick is a very quick and powerful technique for hitting an aggressor where he or she does not expect it. It is similar to the spinning back kick except you pivot further so that your body swings completely around to kick.

Begin in a side-facing horse stance. Pivot on your front foot and swing your body backward toward the aggressor. As your body spins, bend your kicking leg at the knee and turn your head so that you can see the attacker. When the side of the body is facing the attacker, thrust the leg out with a side kick. The heel of your foot should hit the aggressor. Immediately after impact, recoil and then return your kicking foot to the ground.

## Knee Kick

The knee kick is used to strike an aggressor who is standing directly in front of you in the stomach or groin.

Stand in a relaxed position with your feet together. Bring your knee up sharply and hit the aggressor in the stomach or groin. You could also bring your leg up to the side as though throwing a round kick and drive it into the opponent's side.

## Side Kick from the Ground

This kick should be used if an aggressor throws you to the ground and continues to attack. Turn so that you are lying on your side. Place your palms against the ground for support, one on either side of your body. Bend your top knee deeply and draw it toward your chest. Thrust the top leg straight out so that your heel hits the aggressor's knees, groin, or lower stomach. Bring your other leg up, bent, to protect the groin.

# 10

# DODGES AND BLOCKS

A kempo practitioner often seems almost like a serpent because of the way he or she can gracefully move in and around the attacker's guard. Kempo teaches that it is often preferable to avoid punches and kicks rather than make direct contact by blocking them. Evasive movements have several advantages. They save you from having to absorb the energy of the attacker's blows in a block, they frustrate your opponent, and they put you in a better position to counterattack. It is important to keep your body stable while performing the basic dodges and blocks which follow.

## DODGES
### Roll Dodge

Roll dodging is an excellent way to avoid an attacker's technique when you are in a fighting stance. It carries the dual advantage of allowing you to avoid the attacker's punch and putting you in a position to easily counterattack.

Assume a fighting position, such as the back stance. Bend down to the side or to the rear away from your opponent's attack. The motion of a roll dodge must be quick and without hesitation. Keep your legs solidly placed and your eyes on your opponent while performing this evasion.

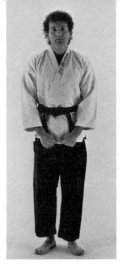

## Backward Dodge

If you are in a natural stance and an opponent throws an attack at your head, step backward with one foot. At the same time bend the top half of your body backward. After the attacker's punch falls short, quickly bend forward as you follow up with a fore-fist punch.

## Circle Dodge

If an opponent throws a kick, simply step to the side with the forward foot. Then swing the rear leg to the side as well. Bend your body away from the attack. After the kick goes by, immediately lunge forward with a counterattack. This dodge is based on the basic circle movement.

## Crouch Dodge from a Natural Stance

As the opponent releases a punch to your head, bend down away from the punch. At the same time, spread your legs and bend your knees deeply into a horse stance so that the punch passes over your head. Immediately follow this with a counterattack to the opponent's body.

## BLOCKS

Kempo practitioners try to avoid being hit by keeping their opponents off balance, by dodging attacks, or by staying out of range of attack. At times, however, it is necessary to block an attack because distancing or dodging are not suitable. Most blocking techniques are done when you are very close to an opponent. Never rely solely on series of blocks to defend yourself. Every time you block a blow, you use up energy. Blocking will eventually wear you down. No matter how skilled you are, it is not always possible to block every attack.

The best way to defend yourself and come out on top is to follow up any block with a series of counterattacks. For that reason, selected blocks taught in this section include counterattack techniques to illustrate possible responses. Practice combining blocks with counters so that you automatically perform them in a real situation. At times, it is a good idea to grab the attacker's limb with your blocking arm to immobilize it while you counterattack. Practice each block alone several times until your form is improving, then include a series of counterattacks. Try to imagine a real opponent as you practice these techniques.

## Inward Block

This can be a very effective forearm block for the middle part of the body. The inward block is delivered from the outside of your body toward the inside. It gets its name from the direction it travels. It can be used in any stance.

If a punch is thrown at your chest while you are in a natural stance, raise your arm on the side of the body that needs to be protected from the punch. Step forward on the same side into a horse stance. At the same time, drive your blocking arm forward, twisting it so that it ends up at the midline of your body with the palm facing you. The opponent's blow should be deflected off the outside of your forearm. As your blocking arm comes into place, pull your other arm down to hip level, palm up, to add extra power to the block. To counter-attack, grab the attacker's punching arm with the blocking hand. Pull downward as you twist your rear hip forward and deliver a reverse punch.

Another alternative is to grab the punching arm and turn it over while your blocking arm pushes downward on the opponent's elbow. Press down and bend the wrist to apply an arm-lock. Whenever possible, try to block in such a way as to throw the attacker off balance and end up to one side of him or her. When you are at one side of the opponent, he or she cannot easily counterattack and will be easy for you to strike at.

## Outward Block

The outward block is a powerful technique that is most often used to protect the middle of the body. It is particularly effective against hand attacks, round kicks, or kicks that travel at an angle. This block can be used in any fighting stance and on either side of your body. It is not necessary to step forward into it. By stepping into a block, however, you do add power to the technique.

Start in a natural stance. To perform this mid-level block, bring the blocking arm across your body as the punch is thrown. Draw your bent arm across your body to just above the opposite hip while stepping forward into a front stance with the leg on the same side. Drive the blocking arm up to meet the attacker's limb as you twist your forearm. The elbow of your blocking arm should not go outside the line of your body. As you swing your blocking arm into place, withdraw the other arm to hip level, palm up. Meet the attacker's blow with the inner edge of the thumb side of your lower forearm. To counterattack, grab the opponent's arm as you fire a reverse punch. Follow up if necessary with a punch to the other side of the body.

## Downward Block

This block can be used to protect the lower part of your body from kicks as well as punches. It is called the downward block because of the direction in which it travels. This block can redirect the attacking limb away from your body. It should be reemphasized that it is preferable to dodge rather than block attacks, especially kicking techniques because of their power.

Assume a basic fighting stance. As the attacker launches a kick, bring your arm downward so that its outer edge deflects the attacking limb. Your arm should be almost fully extended when it makes contact with the opponent's limb. Focus on the point where you want your block to make contact so that you do not miss your target. After you make contact, sweep the attacking limb away from your body and immediately launch a counterattack from the other side of your body. It is not necessary to block with your forward arm. Use the arm that can swing the attacker's body off balance and away from you so your opponent cannot easily launch additional attacks. The key is to block the attacker's technique from the outside so as to turn the opponent away from your body.

## Upper Block and
## Lower Push Block

This is a combination of blocks for protecting against a high and a low attack thrown in very quick succession. Each of these blocking movements can be used separately. They are combined here to get you used to moving very quickly and efficiently. In real combat, an attacker often throws a high attack to distract you from a second attack, which may be low.

Start in any stance. As your opponent throws a punch, bring the arm closest to the punching arm upward to stop the attack. As your arm rises it should twist so that the soft part of the forearm is turned out. Keep your eyes upon your opponent and try to see all of the action. If the attacker follows up with an attack to the lower part of the body, such as a knee kick, bring your other arm downward and push with your palm to stop the blow. After blocking, counter by making your lower hand into a fist and throwing a punch to your attacker's body.

## Fan Block

This block is used in a variety of situations because of its extreme speed and flexibility. It is a circular, fan-like motion. This technique is not a hard movement which stops a blow, but rather a deflective one which redirects the opponent's force.

Begin in a horse stance. Move your rear hand up, palm outward, to block a driving punch. If the aggressor follows with a straight punch, sweep your forward arm in a large circular motion like a fan to push the second attack away. This double movement protects your body from a combination of attacks. To counterattack, drive your rear hand forward with a reverse punch. Follow up with additional techniques if necessary.

## Single-Palm Parry Block

This is one of the most flexible blocks. The hand moves very quickly and smoothly, yet your arms are constantly pointed at the opponent's center line and ready to counterattack. This block is extremely effective against quick, close-range attacks.

If an attacker throws a punch, reach your palm out to push the limb away to the outside. To counter, throw a reverse punch with the other hand.

You can also parry and then recoil and launch an attack with the same hand.

## Knee Block

As the attacker comes in to attack, use your knee to redirect the force. Turn your body to the side to protect the center line of the body. At the same time bring your bent knee up into position to block the attacker's limb.

## Knife-Hand Block

This is a very speedy technique used in a wide range of situations. It is especially useful for protecting the mid-level of the body.

Start in any fighting stance and draw your forward hand up and across so that the palm is facing the ear. The thumb side of the hand should be pointed up. Your other hand should be palm outward. Slash the upraised arm downward as you rotate the wrist so that the edge of the hand contacts the attacker's blow. At the same time, you should quickly withdraw the rear arm back to chest level with the palm facing up.

---

## Sticking Techniques

If your attacker is able to block all of your blows, you want to end that situation. When you throw a technique, you want your attacker's hands tied up so they cannot interfere. Sticking techniques pin or stick an opponent's hands together for a short time.

These techniques are very good when you are close to your opponent. The techniques that follow require a great deal of practice to build speed and timing, however, if they are to work against a well-trained fighter. What follows are only four of many methods of trapping-hand techniques.

## A. Lunging Trap

Assume a basic front stance against an opponent who is in a similar stance. Step forward with a right lunge punch. If your opponent blocks it downward, reach up with your left hand and grab the aggressor's left wrist. Bring it down so that you can attack the opponent's face with a right backfist. If your opponent attempts to block this with his or her right arm, grab it with your right hand. Jerk the person's right arm down and across his or her body so that both of the opponent's arms are trapped together while you deliver a left punch.

## B. Trap for a Driving Punch

This trapping-hand technique starts when your opponent throws a left jab and you block it downward with your left palm. If the person then throws a right reverse punch, reach upward with your right palm and parry it. In the same move, grab and pull the opponent's right arm across his or her left arm to tie the person up. To counterattack, shoot your left arm forward in a driving punch.

## C. The Basic Lead and Trap

Assume a fighting stance facing an attacker in a similar stance. Throw a left driving punch toward your opponent's face. If the person executes an outward block against your punch, grab his or her left wrist with your left hand and bring it down as you punch with your right fist. If your opponent attempts to block your right punch, cross over and grab his or her right wrist with your right hand and pull it so that the person's arms are crossed and tied up. You can then throw a left punch to the face.

## D. Wristlock and Containment

One type of trapping action is the wristlock. This technique does more than momentarily tie up the hands. It contains the aggressor's force by putting pressure on a sensitive part of the arm so that pain rather than your other arm ends the attack.

To execute the basic side wristlock, step to the side of an opponent and grab the closest hand. Insert your elbow in the crook of the aggressor's arm. At the same time, pull his or her hand close to your body and lift it so the person's wrist is bent deeply downward. Press down on the aggressor's wrist with both hands.

At first, practice lock techniques only under supervision by a qualified martial arts instructor. Be sure you are fully warmed up before you practice locks. In practices, never push hard; only simulate the action. Never try to surprise your partner. Always warn him or her before you attempt to perform any technique. Work out a warning system with your partner whereby you can signal each other if a hold begins to hurt.

# 11

# COMBINATIONS

Sometimes a single blow to a sensitive area will stop an attacker. Kempo teaches, however, that you must always have the next technique ready in case the first one does not achieve your goal. Sometimes your first blow may not even land, but be blocked or dodged. In that case you must have another attack on the way or you will lose your momentum and the aggressor may have time to counterattack. At other times, you may want to throw one blow as a distraction for a follow-up technique. Practice linking techniques together so that you can use them spontaneously and effectively in a real fight.

If a blow takes the fight out of an aggressor, don't follow up with other techniques simply because they are part of a combination. Combinations should make you more effective, not brutal.

Practice combinations of movements slowly at first until you develop smooth form. Later, try the same combinations against a punching bag. After you are familiar with the movements and have developed proper form and timing, you may practice them with a partner. Have your partner dodge or block the first and second attacks, just as an opponent might do, and then let you "score" with your last technique. This is excellent preparation for self-defense and sporting contests.

Practice landing a series of blows only on a bag, not on a partner. Develop a sense of the distance at which you can put the maximum power into each blow. Certain combinations only work when an opponent is at a specific range. It is a good idea to vary the levels of the techniques thrown in a combination. This keeps the opponent confused. Do not throw combinations mechanically—adapt them to the situation.

The following combinations of techniques are for your initial practice. As you grow in skill, you may add others.

## Front Kick, Driving Punch, Right Reverse Punch

Throw a front kick with your rear leg at the opponent's body. Immediately afterwards, return the foot to where it started and launch a left driving punch with your forward arm. Follow up with a right reverse punch.

## Front Kick, Side Kick

Launch a quick front kick with your forward leg to the opponent's body. Immediately after this kick, drop your foot to the ground and bring your rear leg up while you twist your body to the side. Launch your side kick at the attacker's upper body.

## Backfist, Foot Sweep, Forefist Punch

Lead off with a backfist strike with your forward arm toward the opponent's head. As your arm recoils from the strike, move your rear leg forward and behind the attacker's forward leg in a sweeping motion. Your advancing leg should knock the opponent off balance so that he or she cannot easily oppose your last technique, a forefist punch off the forward side.

## Palm-up Punch, Left Circle Punch, High Guard Quarter-Turn Punch

From a high guard stance launch a right palm-up punch to the opponent's stomach. As he or she begins to block it, shoot a left circle punch at the opponent's head. After hitting, quickly retract your arm and drive your right hand out in a high guard quarter-turn or reverse punch.

## Left Driving Punch, Left Backfist, High Guard Quarter-Turn Punch

This combination of hand movements is very effective for long-range attacks. Lead with a left driving punch. Follow up quickly by coiling your hand back with a twist in preparation for a backfist strike. Then snap your hand out in a backfist followed by a right high guard quarter-turn or reverse punch to the head. The quicker the series of blows the more likely they are to land.

## Side Kick, Round Kick

From a side-facing horse stance, lift up your left forward leg and throw a side kick to the opponent's body. Drop your foot back down and bring your other leg up in a coiled position to the side of your body. Shoot a right round kick to the opponent's ribs. Return to a balanced stance.

## Cross Step, Backfist, Sweep

Begin in a side-facing horse stance. Cross-step to place your back leg behind your front and shoot a backfist out to the opponent's head. Next, slide your front foot behind the opponent's forward leg and sweep the opponent across your leg to the ground with your forward arm.

## Side Kick, Round Kick, Back Kick

From a side-facing horse stance launch a side kick with your forward leg. Return that foot to the ground as you lift the other leg and throw a right round kick to the opponent's side. Then set your foot down to the side as your other leg coils toward your chest. You should now be turned partially away from the opponent. Quickly shoot out a back kick to the opponent's body. This technique must be done very quickly and only against an opponent who backs up after your round kick. If the attacker does not back up, you will be too close and too vulnerable to a counterattack to use the back kick.

## Front Kick, Spinning Back Kick

Throw a low front kick with your forward leg to the opponent's torso. If your attacker retreats, place your foot on the ground off to the side and turn your body so that your back is facing the opponent. Lift up the opposite leg toward your chest and shoot out a back kick.

## Palm-up Punch, Circle Punch, Forefist Punch

If you see an opening for a punch in your opponent's solar plexus area, drive your rear hand toward it in a palm-up punch. If the opponent moves to block the punch, recoil your arm slightly and use the same fist to throw a circle punch to the side of the head. Follow up quickly with a forefist or driving punch with the front hand.

# 12

# EFFECTIVE KEMPO STRATEGY

Many people imagine that training in kempo consists of breaking a stack of boards. The obvious implication is that brute force can overcome any opponent. This is not true, however. A strong kempo practitioner not only has power and speed but, more importantly, is able to outmaneuver an opponent. You must develop your mental power from the start of your training. Concentration and clear thinking are key factors in the development of any kempo practitioner.

The goal of a kempo student is not to destroy an adversary, but to end the fight quickly. Kempo practitioners believe that the better they are, the less damage they will have to do to subdue an opponent. That means that you must develop proper techniques and responses rather than relying on brute force. You are encouraged to learn fighting strategy from the beginning of training along with techniques. Every aggressor will be different, so you must be flexible and able to adapt to the opponent that you face.

This chapter explains general fighting strategy that can be used to defeat an opponent. Most of the basic principles apply in both sports contests and in real fights. Learn them well and you will benefit. Before entering a sports contest, however, read the rules to see what useful limitations have been put on strategy or technique.

Kempo strategy and techniques should not be used to pick fights. The very essence of kempo is the development of harmony in relations with others. The moment a person improperly uses kempo he or she forfeits the right to think of himself or herself as an outstanding practitioner. Try to avoid fights. However, if this is not possible because of the other person's aggression, you must think ahead and plan your fight.

You must practice your techniques, study their application, and adjust them to your own needs. You will learn to take great pride not only in executing techniques properly, but in choosing the proper techniques to use in each circumstance. The fascinating puzzle of choosing techniques and responses to an opponent's action is one of the challenges that makes kempo exciting.

As you read through the chapter try to think of the practical applications of the points and principles outlined in it.

# BASIC PRINCIPLES OF KEMPO STRATEGY

## 1. Keep calm.

You must remain calm when facing an attacker. Your mind should be as smooth as the surface of a still pool of water so that you will easily be able to spot all of the attacker's

moves and to mount the appropriate response. When your mind is distracted and your concentration is broken, you will not see your opponent's moves as clearly nor protect yourself or counterattack as surely.

## 2. Use your mind, not your emotions.

Don't allow self-doubt to diminish your response. A bully who tries to psyche you out by his or her image, reputation, or actions may in reality be very insecure. If bullies were really

tough, they wouldn't have to pick fights to show how brave they are. Show by your attitude that you will not be intimidated. Look your opponent straight in the eye with an expression that clearly says, "I do not fear you or the challenge of a confrontation." Do not think of losing but instead concentrate on the opponent and his or her actions so you can respond instantly. This may discourage the adversary before he or she actually moves forward to attack.

## 3. Control the situation.

Size up the aggressor, check out the location, and imagine where things could go wrong. Try to maneuver into a place where you can best take advantage of your skills. For example, if you like to throw kicks and keep the opponent at a distance, make sure that the space allows for those techniques to be used.

Keep your eyes on your opponent and do not turn your back unless you are sure there is no chance for the person to attack you. Many a person has started to take off a coat and been hit while doing so.

Never walk into a strange place or out into an alley where you might be caught off guard. Keep your stance strong, yet flexible enough to move quickly if need be. If you understand the situation you will have more confidence in the outcome. As you watch your opponent, try to also scan the room for hazards and see whether any other people might join the opponent. If you have carefully controlled the situation and developed a strategy, you will feel far more self-confident. This will be translated to your opponent as greater power, which may discourage him or her. If a fight does occur, you will be ready and better able handle it.

**4. Watch the opponent's actions.**

Observe everything your opponent

does. Even the smallest movements could signal an attack or an opening. For example, if the aggressor transfers weight from one leg to the other, he or she may be preparing to throw a kick. Practice sensing what an opponent will do next with a partner. Your vision should cover everything the way that moonlight covers the ground. Nothing falls outside the moon's range, nor should the kempo practitioner miss anything. Distractions that interfere with your insight into the aggressor's movements are similar to clouds that

block the moon. You must reflect on what you see without distraction. If you do this, you will not easily be caught off guard and can find openings to attack.

**5. Size up an opponent.**

Don't rush in to attack at first, unless there is a clear opening. Instead,

try to judge your opponent's size, balance, openings, and style of fighting. Try to find out as much about the person as possible. Check your opponent's stance and posture. Try to figure out what advantages and disadvantages he or she would have in a confrontation. If a fight does occur, test the attacker's reactions with fakes to determine how he or she reacts to certain situations. Make sure your fake is realistic enough to cause a reaction. If the aggressor throws a punch you will know that he or she is more oriented towards hand techniques; if your opponent backs up and starts to kick, you will know he or she prefers long-distance foot attacks.

Once you have determined the person's weakness, set the opponent up. Don't just react, but use combinations of techniques to score. Think of

a strategy that will catch your opponent by surprise.

Use fakes that are the opposite of the technique that you will use to score: fake high and attack low; throw a fake to one side and score with a blow to the other. If you lead with a straight fake then follow through with a circular attack. The more time you spend practicing fakes with actual techniques the more self-confident you will be.

Strategy is the key to winning a difficult fight. Make sure that you fight your fight: use the techniques that you feel most comfortable performing. Don't let your opponent force you into fighting the way that he or she prefers.

## 6. Consider range in choosing techniques.

The distance between you and an opponent is an important consideration in any fight. Four ranges can be defined.

*Safety range* is where an opponent's longest limb cannot reach you. When

*Safety range*

you are at this range you are safe from attack. At the beginning of a fight it is very important to keep this distance so an opponent cannot catch you off guard.

*Long range* is where your kicks and some longer punches such as lunge punches or high guard quarter-turn punches may reach an opponent. Some of your opponent's techniques will also reach you. This distance is ideal for those who prefer to use these longer techniques. Many karate styles emphasize techniques performed at this range. However, avoid this distance if you are shorter than your opponent. A taller opponent will have longer arms and legs and can hit you when you cannot reach to do so in return.

*Close range*

*Long range*

*Close range* is where either opponent will clearly be able to hit the other with punches such as a round punch or palm-up punch. If you have the shorter reach you may elect to go to close range. At this distance, a smaller person can move in quickly to hammer a larger opponent and then pull back. If your opponent is similar to you in size and strength, sticking techniques are ideal for tying the person up at this range.

*Close range*

*Holding range*

*Holding range* is where the opponent is very close so he or she can easily grab you to apply a hold or execute a throw. This distance can be useful if you are skillful at such techniques but it can be very dangerous for a smaller, weaker person up against a larger, more powerful opponent.

Kempo teaches techniques that are useful at each range and in a fight you must pick those techniques that fit your opponent, your strategy, and the range. The better you control the situation by making the opponent fight your kind of fight, the more comfortable you will feel. Beginning students tend to fight in the close range or holding range and this may prove a disaster if he or she is weaker at grappling or is caught by surprise with a punch. Try to start at safety range

until you have sized up your opponent and developed a plan. When you pick fighting techniques, consider what range they should be launched from and the range at which your opponent is weakest. If you close from one range to another, move quickly and try to execute a fighting technique while doing so. Do not stay at one range unless you clearly have the advantage. Move in and out to confuse the opponent and use each range's advantages.

### 7. Disrupt an opponent's balance.

Both before and during a fight you must observe your opponent's stance. If the aggressor's center of gravity is high and he or she is unbalanced, you may choose to throw or sweep the person. When the attacker starts to lift one foot to move forward and transfer weight, he or she may be open to a disruption of balance. If, on the other hand, your opponent has a

deep, well-balanced stance and a low center of gravity, a throw may be difficult. In this case you should instead move around the person quickly with a series of punches, taking advantage of the opponent's lack of mobility. Do not telegraph what you plan to do, but perform your throw or disruption of balance without hesitation. If an opponent is not off balance to begin with, you can manipulate his or her balance by pushing or pulling the person or by your movement. For example, you can throw a punch which will force an opponent to back up quickly. If the adversary moves back off balance, immediately attack to take advantage of it.

Some opponents will attempt to push you. Instead of resisting, pull as your opponent pushes. This will use the adversary's weight and power against him or her so that the person will be thrown forward off balance. On the other hand, if your opponent pulls, you should push. This will use the person's weight and power to force him or her backward off balance.

You can usually get a good idea of an opponent's balance by watching the direction in which his or her body bends. If the upper half of the person's body is bent to the left, he or she may be off balance in that direction. If you attack to force your opponent further to the left, he or she may be so off balance that you can easily counterattack with your hands or a throw. If an opponent is forced onto one leg, you can kick the person's stationary leg out from under

to knock the opponent to the ground. Generally the direction in which the head is tilted affects the way the body will go. A person whose face is tilted downward may be more easily pulled forward. A good fighter takes advantage of any changes in balance to come out on top.

## 8. Use movement as a defensive weapon.

Many an aggressor has been frustrated by a seemingly weaker person who moves around so he or she cannot be hit. As frustration mounts, mistakes accumulate and these can cause openings for attack. As you move, you want to set up an opponent so you can hit the person but he or she can't hit you. Vary your movements so that you are not predictable. Stay balanced when you move.

There are two basic types of movement, linear and circular. Both are used in kempo. Linear techniques generally move in a straight line forward, from side to side, or backward. They are very useful when an attacker is the same size as you and leaves clear openings. Straight-line movement is fast and efficient. Be careful, however, to cover up, hit, and move out quickly. Watch out for the skillful opponent who appears to leave an opening only to draw you into a trap.

Circular movement allows you to move around an opponent and attack from an angle. If you use circular movement properly, you can hit your opponent's side or back while staying outside the person's effective range. Practice sidestepping and moving in at an angle to attack an opponent's side or back. A circular movement may so confuse an opponent that you can set the person up for an attack just by moving to a certain position.

As your opponent shifts position in response to your movement, be prepared for quick action. Decide whether to use a straight-line attack or to try circling. You must not move in predictable patterns if you are to take advantage of the opponent.

## 9. Keep techniques simple.

Use lead techniques such as a driving punch or backfist strike. In a real fight, stick with basic techniques; don't try something fancy that may not work for you. The best techniques are not always dramatic, but they can consistently generate power and force.

Avoid flashy techniques and rely on punches and kicks that you can do almost automatically.

Don't use spinning techniques unless these conditions exist: it is clear that the opponent is open; you have great skill in the technique; the opponent is weakened; the opponent is retreating; there is a great deal of space to move in; and the opponent cannot counterattack easily while you are kicking. Unless all of these conditions are met, even a highly skilled kempo practitioner would generally not use the technique in a real fight. This is because turning your back on an opponent often means disaster. Spinning techniques are best used in sporting contests in which there is plenty of room and there are limitations on the use of force.

In executing some techniques there are certain openings that you must carefully protect. For example, when throwing round kicks be ready to protect the groin area.

Kicks aimed at head level are not usually practical in a real fight. Your body may not be adequately stretched out and such a technique may leave you off balance. Although in sporting contests it wouldn't be allowed, in a street fight an opponent might rush in and jam your high kick to force you to the ground. Also, the head is a small target for a kick and very hard when hit. The chest and stomach areas are larger and softer targets. It is highly recommended that you aim only at lower targets with your feet and use your hands against areas above the solar plexus.

## 10. Use the element of surprise.

Even powerful opponents can be defeated if caught off guard by a strike to a sensitive area. Try to keep the

opponent off balance, mentally as well as physically. This can sometimes be done by distracting the opponent.

Yelling, throwing an object, or executing a fake are all examples of distractions. Often a high hand technique is an excellent distraction for a low kick, which is the real attack. In practice sessions, execute hand and foot movements in quick succession so you can develop expertise in switching from high to low attacks. In the midst of a fight, an opponent sometimes will defend one side of his or her body more than the other. By shifting your stance, you may position yourself so you can throw a technique to hit your adversary on the side he or she is not used to protecting. Do whatever you can to make your actions unpredictable and leave the opponent confused.

## 11. Use a variety of fighting techniques.

It is not possible to rely on one technique to end a fight. Therefore, it is important to throw a combination of techniques. Timing is important for success in penetrating your opponent's guard. Never just throw combinations hoping they will hit; instead,

look ahead for patterns or openings that can be exploited. Aim your combinations at specific targets. Be careful not to repeat even the best combinations too often. The opponent will recognize them and take advantage of this knowledge.

A good time to throw a combination is at the moment your opponent is thinking of something else, such as during an advance, response to a fake, or even change in stance.

Combinations can also be extremely useful for defense. Watch the aggressor carefully and start your techniques after the opponent's attack, just as the attacker changes range or retreats.

Even the rhythm of your delivery must be varied. Don't develop a habit of stepping back a couple of times before executing a kick, or stepping to the side before throwing a punch. Throw your combinations quickly from the correct range so as not to telegraph to the opponent what to expect next.

## HANDLING DIFFERENT TYPES OF OPPONENTS

People can be classified in groups according to the way they prefer to fight. There are six basic types of individuals, and certain responses are recommended for each of these types. Keep in mind, however, that an opponent may not fall into only one "type," but may share characteristics of different types. You will have to judge your opponent's tactics and combine responses for whatever characteristics he or she displays.

If you are more powerful, you may want to close in very quickly to grab the person and take him or her down once you have found a break in the opponent's rhythm. If your opponent relies on movement, gradually move back and forth to cut off the person's space. He or she may become frustrated and make mistakes when feeling trapped at close range. Presence of mind and a refusal to be impressed by flashy techniques can be real advantages in dealing with such an individual.

## The Flashy Fighter

This individual throws fancy techniques very quickly to impress or intimidate his or her opponent. You must not allow such an individual to have an effect upon you. Hold back and judge the opponent's weaknesses. You will often find that his or her impressive techniques are so seriously flawed that you can easily take advantage of them. At the beginning of a fight with such a person, stay in a strong, high-guard position and keep moving around your opponent. Try to dodge any attack. After you have found your opponent's weaknesses, quickly move in to deliver hard punches to sensitive spots and then withdraw. Concentrate on the openings and try to take advantage of them. Individuals of this type are often open to attacks to the lower parts of the body, such as the knees or shins.

## The Kicking Specialist

Some persons take great pride in fighting from a long range with their feet. They can be highly effective and you must do whatever possible to neutralize their skill. It is often best to carry the fight to a close range where short hand techniques make your opponent uncomfortable. If the opponent blocks, try to trap his or her hands with sticking hand techniques. Just being in close can take the edge off the kicking specialist's fight. Do not try to match kicking techniques, unless you are equally as skillful. When such an opponent throws high kicks you may be able to throw him or her off balance. However, it is important that when you close distance you also throw punches so your opponent cannot hit you in the interval. Another approach is to dodge a kick and follow through with your own kick to the opponent's supporting leg. Kicking specialists are often greatly discouraged by a kick to the shin, knee, or groin. While moving around, keep your hands high to protect your head, and keep in the safety range or close range to minimize your opponent's strengths.

**The Heavy Puncher**

When fighting a very powerful opponent it is important that you do not get so close that the person can easily grab or punch you. To avoid this, stay at long or safety range most of the time. Be careful not to let your opponent cut off the space so that the person can corner you and use his or her superior power. A great physique should not be intimidating, however, since the puncher cannot hit you if you are out of range. If this individual is not skillful, he or she may not be able to put all of his or her power into a technique anyway.

Watch carefully and when the

puncher is getting set to throw a punch, move quickly to disrupt his or her rhythm. Circle your opponent so that he or she is off balance. Try to attack at an angle so that the puncher cannot easily grab you or hit you. Mix straight-line attacks with attacks to the opponent's side. Throw a quick set of punches and move out. Vary the angle of your attacks throughout the confrontation so as to be unpredictable. Make sure lead techniques like driving punches and backfists are very quick and crisp so your opponent cannot grab or counter your technique. Do not try to slug it out or grapple with a person with far superior strength.

If your opponent relies on having one side of his or her body forward, shift stances to place your other foot forward so that you catch him or her off guard with a different body position. Be careful to quickly execute your technique and withdraw. If a power puncher does change position to respond to your move, you may have put the person at a disadvantage. For example, a person whose main weapon is a powerful right hand loses some of his or her power advantage when he or she shifts to put the right side in front. When you know an opponent is particularly strong on one side, try to move to make it nearly impossible for the person to get at you with that side. To overcome the powerhouse opponent you must stay away from him or her most of the time and move in only when it can be done quickly and by surprise.

**The Aggressive Fighter**

Certain kinds of bullies may have very little skill, yet their continual barrage of attacks wears down a defender. Stay at safety range from such

an opponent until a pattern of attack can be seen. Keep the aggressor away with driving punches and side kicks until you are ready to mount your own attack. A windmill attack (wild punches of one arm followed by the other) is often the aggressor's strategy. If this is your opponent's style, hit any opening in the middle of such an attack.

If your opponent puts his or her head down and starts swinging, kick hard into any opening. A kick lets you stay at a distance, so that you can hit the bully without him or her being able to get at you. One of the best kicks for this is a side kick. In practice sessions, allow your partner to charge as you execute a side kick. Another tactic that is often useful is to side-step, hit with a quick barrage of hand attacks on the opponent's side, and then withdraw. When attacking, it may sometimes be useful to step to the side before moving in so you can attack the opponent at an angle to surprise him or her. Be careful not to let your opponent cut off your space or corner you so that he or she can fight at close range. If he or she manages to close in, use your knees or elbows. Watch the opponent's movements carefully for instability. Try to take advantage of the opponent's loss of balance with a throw. Many aggressive fighters, when faced with an intelligent opponent who does not easily cave in, get discouraged and ease up.

**The Cautious Strategist**

Some individuals are cautious. They

wait until you make a mistake and then counterattack. This opponent can be dangerous because he or she relies upon mind instead of muscle to win. Do not lead with the types of techniques that your opponent will expect, such as a backfist or front kick. Instead, fake and draw the strategist into action. When your opponent moves, counter with a quick combination of attacks on your own and withdraw.

Try to keep the opponent off balance. Stay to your opponent's left or right and attack from an angle. This adversary will often become dismayed when you continually dodge attacks.

If you can see a predictable pattern of response to your movements, repeat the action and hit your opponent while he or she is moving. Try to see if your opponent can be faked with a circular attack, such as a ridge hand

strike, and then caught off guard with a straight-line driving punch or front kick. Once you have found a potential opening for a certain type of attack, launch it quickly in combination with other movements. The faster your combinations, the more difficult they are to counter.

One good blow may end the fight, but a succession of successful blows will always take their toll on even the most powerful of individuals. If the aggressor is not a great deal stronger, sticking techniques can be very effective. Be unpredictable and you will eventually frustrate the counterattacker and force him or her to make a rash mistake. If you can get such a person flustered and follow through quickly with a series of blows it may very well end the confrontation.

**The Skilled Fighter**

This individual is the most difficult to fight because he or she will not only throw a combination of punches and kicks but will also apply strategy. Fortunately, very few skilled fighters are met in street fights. Skillful, confident individuals don't need to pick fights to prove themselves. However, if you do have to face such a person, do not be intimidated. Even the most skillful individuals leave openings and are off balance at times.

Size your opponent up just like you would any other opponent and move in and out to take advantage of the proper range. Try to approach the opponent at an angle to catch him or her by surprise and make defense dif-

may be too weak to counter. The key concern is your presence of mind and your ability to keep the skillful fighter so off balance mentally that the person cannot use all of his or her skill.

## The Grappler

Some individuals have great skill in wrestling, judo, or other grappling arts. Do not underestimate the danger of such an individual. Although kempo includes some very sophisticated movements for close and holding range that are taught to advanced students, they are beyond the scope of this book. If you are not particularly capable in grappling and want to improve your skills, consider taking a judo or jujitsu course. The more you

ficult. Fake to keep your opponent from following through with a smooth set of combinations. He or she may not be used to this and may leave openings due to frustration.

Do not try to match techniques or exchange punches and kicks. Instead rely upon hitting the fighter when he or she is open. The shins and knees are difficult to protect. Attacks to these areas should be combined with follow-up techniques at angles where your opponent cannot easily reach you. Try to dodge or sidestep attacks and follow up with quick series of punches.

If the opponent tires, you may move in close and use a sweep or wristlock to further take the fight out of the opponent. Use such techniques only if you are familiar with them and the opponent has shown that he or she know about holding or grappling range techniques the more confident and better able you will be to defend yourself in a fight.

If you are not skillful in this area, you must be very careful to keep at long range most of the time and to move into close range only to punch at an angle to an opponent. Never move straight forward into an attacker's grabbing arms. Although a powerful punch may drop one opponent, the same blow may have a different effect on another adversary. Some grappling opponents may be willing to take a blow while moving in to grab you and take you to the ground. That is why when first sizing up such an individual you should move around your opponent trying to spot the best opening. Strike at the side of the opponent so it is difficult for him or her to get at you.

Avoid high kicks that will leave you off balance. Any kicks should be very quick and no higher than knee level. If you are forced into very close proximity, immediately locate a sensitive spot, hit quickly and hard, and withdraw. If the aggressor charges, try to sidestep or dodge and follow up with a fast series of punches.

Try to off balance the attacker as much as possible with movement. An off-balance aggressor cannot easily attack or counter your techniques.

When an opponent tries to clinch, push him or her away, or use the knee kick, an elbow strike, or a short, low kick to the shins. If the opponent grabs you, his or her grasp may be broken by bending the little finger back, hitting a sensitive spot with a great deal of power, or even pinching. Do not become disheartened in dealing with such an individual. Use a strategy that keeps you out of range and lets you throw techniques at the opponent from a distance.

The strategic concerns outlined in this chapter are only a beginning, not the final word in the development of a kempo practitioner. As you learn various techniques and movements, try to think about their uses in a real fight. As you practice techniques, imagine an opponent of a particular type and how you would handle that opponent. The better your application of techniques and strategy in practice, the more likely you will be able to use them in a real fight.

When performed properly, kempo practice can be not only helpful for self-defense, but also enlightening. In a practice session try to follow proper form in a slow and even manner. Practice is not an actual fight or a test of how much punishment you can take, but a chance to develop yourself physically, mentally, and spiritually. It is also a time when you may work with a partner to improve your health and your self-defense skills.

It is important to take proper safety precautions to avoid injury. The following safety rules will reduce the risk of injury and increase your enjoyment of practice sessions.

1. Be sure to do warm-up exercises before each session. At the end of training a cool-down set of exercises should also be performed.

2. Do not stretch your muscles too much at any given time. It is better to stretch a little each day and improve slowly than to do too much all at once and injure yourself.

3. Do not hit your partner. Stop your punches, strikes, or kicks at least one inch (2.5 centimeters) from your partner's body. When first learning to spar with a partner, it is a good idea to use safety equipment such as a mouth guard, and a groin cup for males. A variety of other protective gear is available to make practice safer. Use a punching bag when you want to practice landing a kick, punch, or strike. Only advanced students, with an instructor's permission and supervision, are allowed to hit one another with punches or kicks.

4. Never surprise your partner with a throw, sweep, lock, or hold in practice. Be sure that he or she is ready before you start these techniques.

5. Do not practice throws or sweeps with a partner who does not know how to fall properly.

6. Always practice throws or sweeps on a thick mat designed for falling.

7. Make sure both you and your partner are loose, warm, and well stretched before practicing any locking techniques or holds. Never apply any hold with full pressure.

8. Get your partner's consent before applying any lock or hold in practice. Do not force a hold on your partner.

9. Work out a warning system with your partner by which you can signal each other if a hold or lock begins to cause discomfort.

10. When first learning a lock, hold, throw, or sweep, do it slowly and carefully, under the guidance of a qualified person.